PHOTO

ALBUM

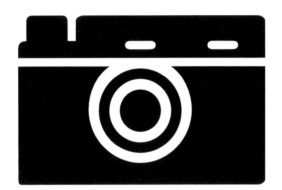

Belongs to

Place _____

Date _____ Title _____

Notes

_____

_____

_____

_____

_____

Place

Title

Date

Notes

Place _____

Date _____ Title _____

Notes

_____
_____
_____
_____
_____

Place

Title

Date

Notes

Place _____

Date _____ Title _____

Notes

_____

_____

_____

_____

_____

Place _____

_____

_____

Title _____

_____

_____

Date _____

Notes

_____

_____

_____

_____

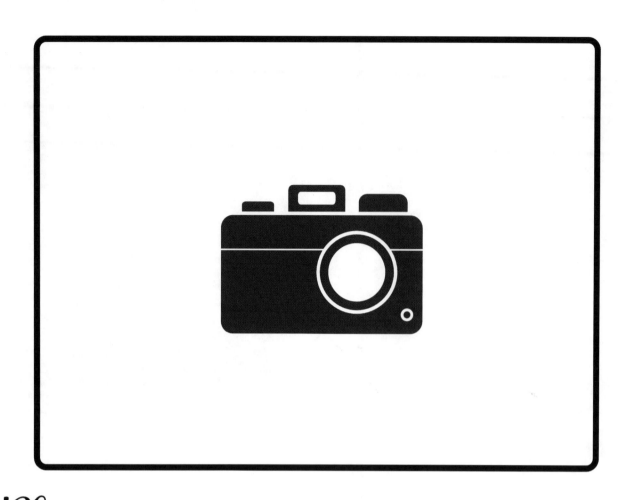

Place ————————————————————————

Date ———————— *Title* ———————————

Notes

————————————————————————————
————————————————————————————
————————————————————————————
————————————————————————————
————————————————————————————

Place _____

_____

_____

Title _____

_____

_____

Date _____

_____

Notes

_____

_____

_____

_____

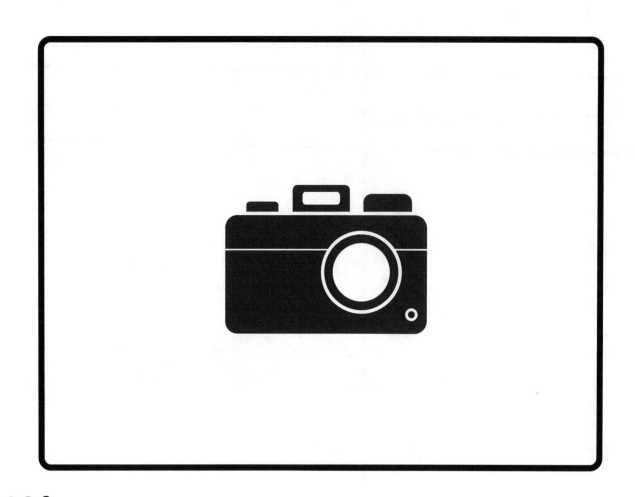

Place _____

Date _____ Title _____

Notes

_____
_____
_____
_____
_____

Place _____
_____
_____

Title _____
_____
_____

Date _____

Notes

_____
_____
_____
_____

Place _____

Date _____ Title _____

Notes

_____

_____

_____

_____

_____

Place _____

_____

_____

Title _____

_____

_____

Date _____

Notes

_____

_____

_____

_____

Place _____

Date _____ Title _____

Notes

_____
_____
_____
_____
_____

Place

Title

Date

Notes

Place ⸻

Date ⸻ Title ⸻

Notes

Place

Title

Date

Notes

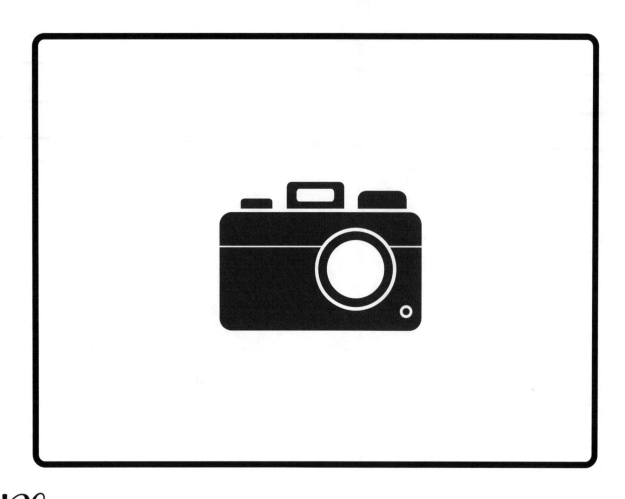

Place _____

Date _____ Title _____

Notes

_____

_____

_____

_____

_____

Place _____

_____

_____

Title _____

_____

_____

Date _____

Notes

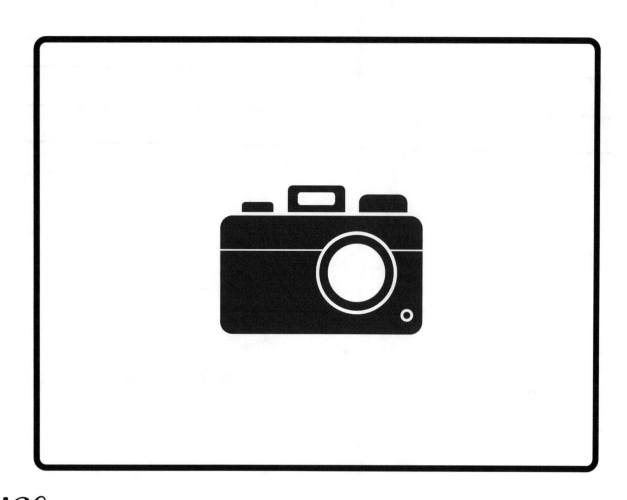

Place _____

Date _____ Title _____

Notes
_____
_____
_____
_____
_____

Place

_____

_____

_____

Title

_____

_____

Date

_____

Notes

_____

_____

_____

_____

Place _____

Date _____ Title _____

Notes

Place

Title

Date

Notes

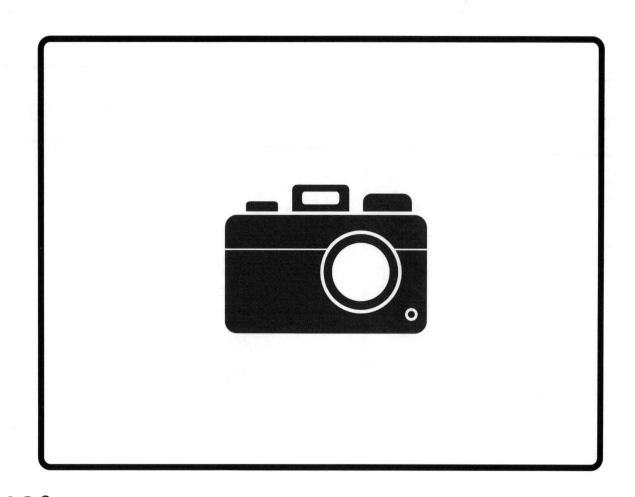

Place ——————————————————

Date ———— Title ————————

Notes

Place

Title

Date

Notes

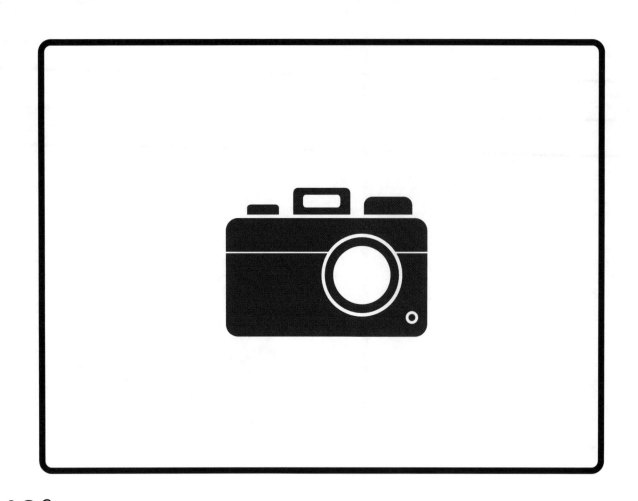

Place _____

Date _____ Title _____

Notes

_____

_____

_____

_____

_____

Place _____

_____

_____

Title _____

_____

_____

Date _____

Notes

_____

_____

_____

_____

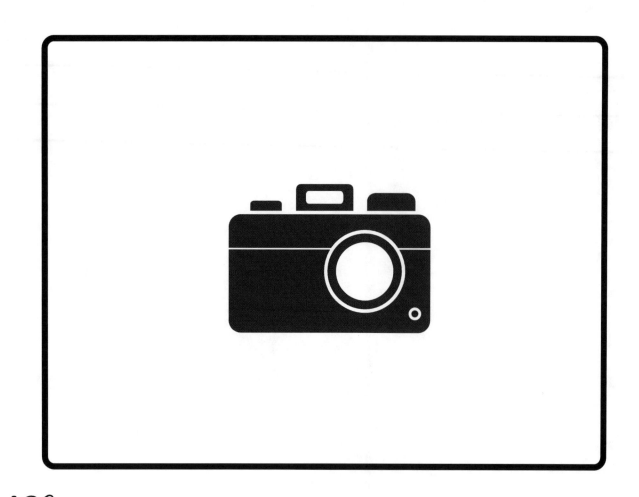

Place _____

Date _____ Title _____

Notes

_____

_____

_____

_____

_____

Place

Title

Date

Notes

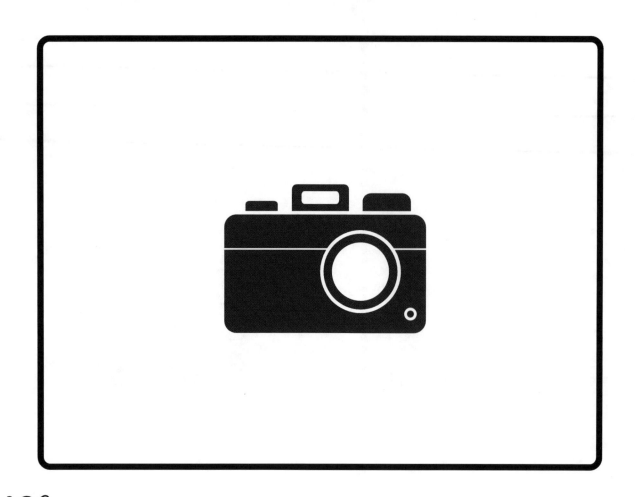

Place _____

Date _____ Title _____

Notes

_____

_____

_____

_____

_____

Place

_____

Title

_____

Date

_____

Notes

_____

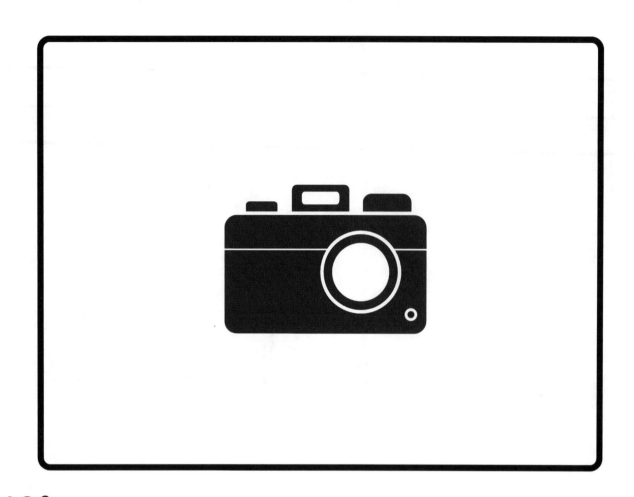

Place _____

Date _____ Title _____

Notes

_____

_____

_____

_____

_____

Place

_____

_____

Title

_____

_____

Date

Notes

_____

_____

_____

_____

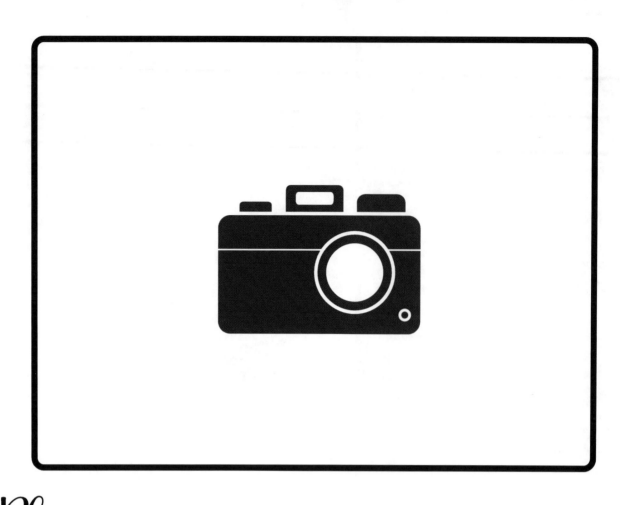

Place _____

Date _____ Title _____

Notes

_____
_____
_____
_____
_____

Place _____

_____

_____

Title _____

_____

Date _____

Notes

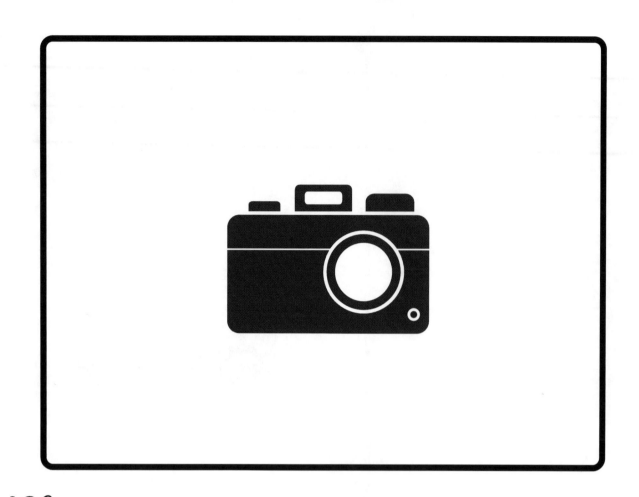

Place _____

Date _____ Title _____

Notes

_____
_____
_____
_____
_____

Place

Title

Date

Notes

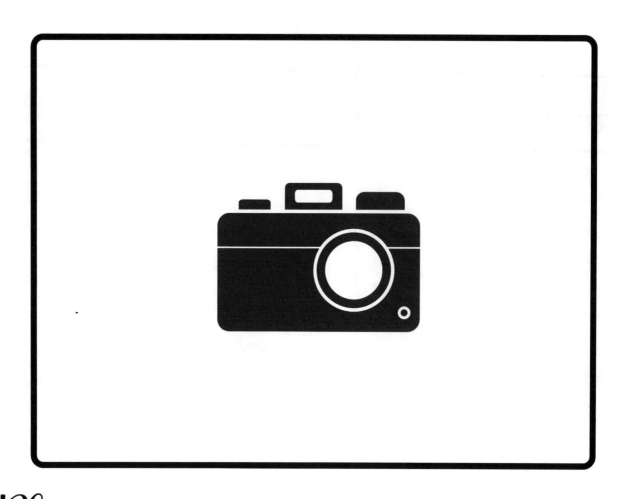

Place _____

Date _____ Title _____

Notes

_____

_____

_____

_____

_____

Place

Title

Date

Notes

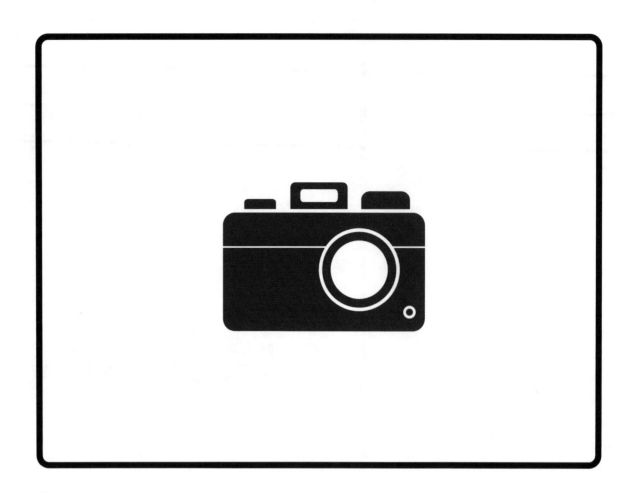

Place _____

Date _____ Title _____

Notes

Place

Title

Date

Notes

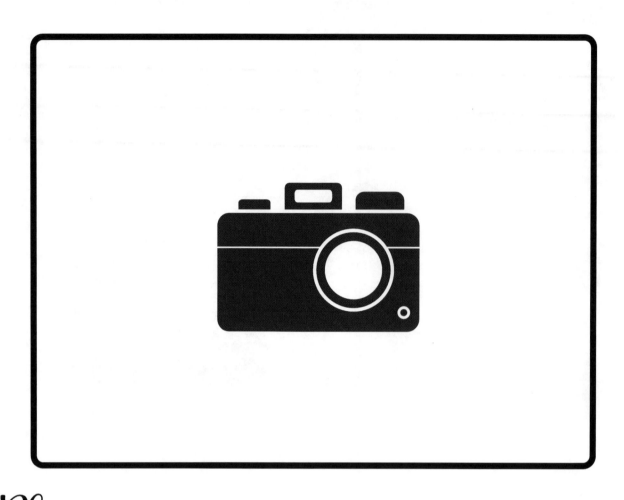

Place ————————————————————

Date ——————— Title ——————————

Notes

————————————————————————————

————————————————————————————

————————————————————————————

————————————————————————————

————————————————————————————

Place _____

_____

Title _____

_____

Date _____

Notes

_____

_____

_____

_____

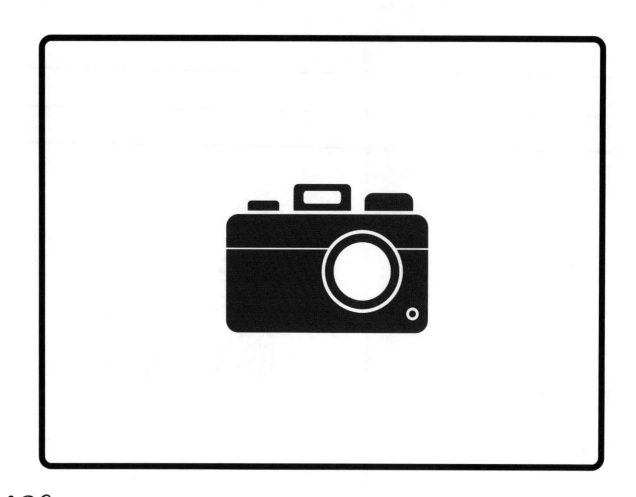

Place ⎯⎯⎯⎯⎯⎯⎯⎯⎯⎯⎯⎯⎯⎯⎯⎯⎯⎯⎯⎯

Date ⎯⎯⎯⎯⎯⎯⎯⎯ Title ⎯⎯⎯⎯⎯⎯⎯⎯

Notes

Place ....

....

....

Title ....

....

....

Date ....

Notes

....

....

....

....

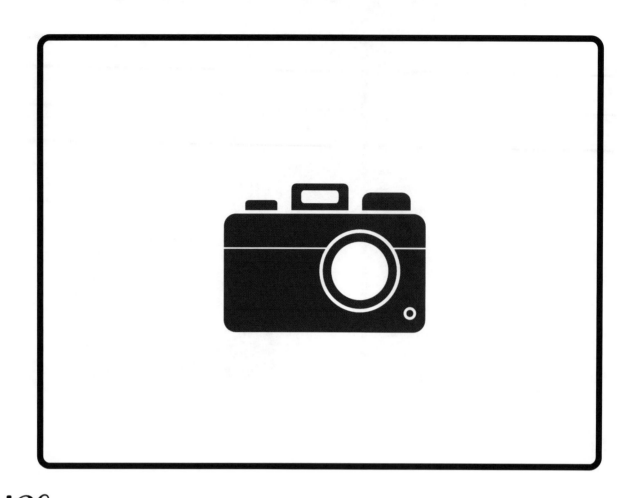

Place ———————————————————

Date ————— *Title* —————

Notes

————————————————————

————————————————————

————————————————————

————————————————————

————————————————————

Place

_____

Title

_____

Date

_____

Notes

_____

_____

_____

_____

Place

Date   *Title*

Notes

Place _____

_____

_____

Title _____

_____

Date _____

Notes
_____

_____

_____

_____

Place _____

Date _____ Title _____

Notes

Place

Title

Date

Notes

Place _____

Date _____ Title _____

Notes

_____
_____
_____
_____
_____

Place

Title

Date

Notes

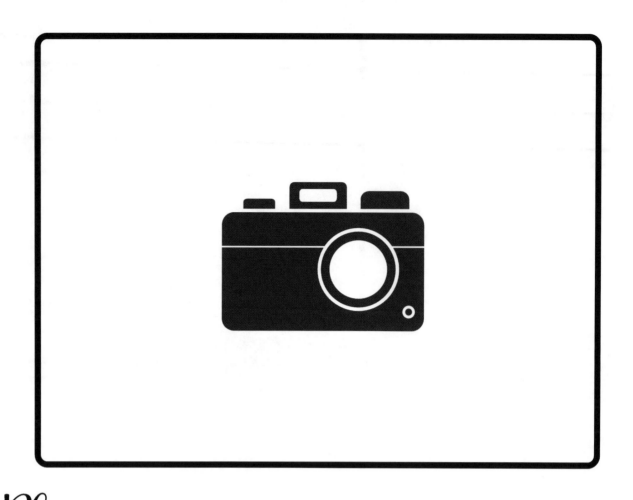

Place _____

Date _____ Title _____

Notes

Place

Title

Date

Notes

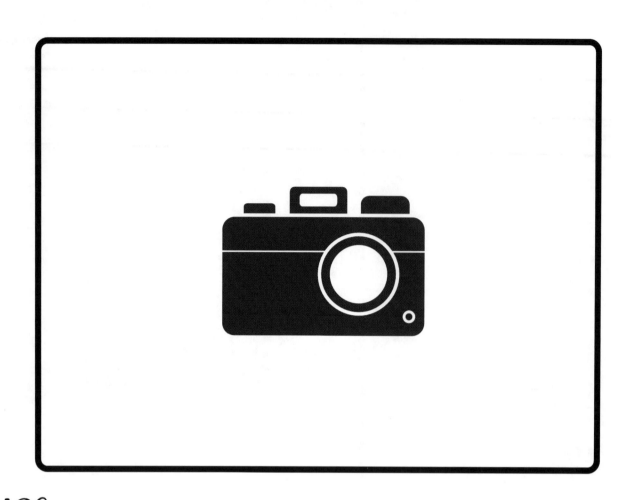

Place ⎯⎯⎯⎯⎯⎯⎯⎯⎯⎯⎯⎯⎯⎯⎯⎯⎯⎯⎯

Date ⎯⎯⎯⎯⎯⎯ Title ⎯⎯⎯⎯⎯⎯⎯⎯⎯⎯

Notes

Place _____

Title _____

Date _____

Notes

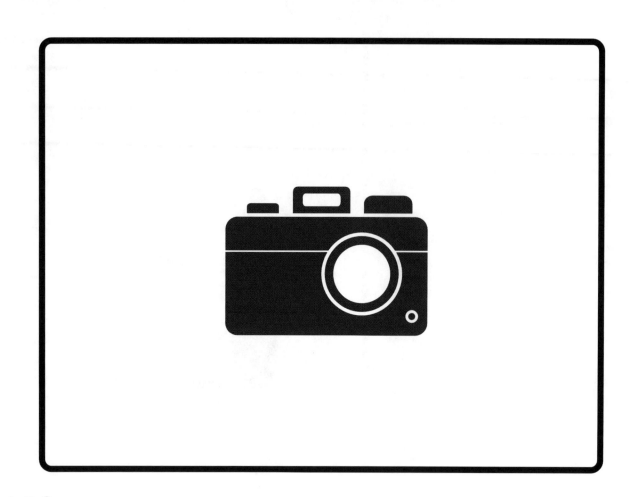

Place ———————————————————

Date ——————— *Title* ———————

Notes

———————————————————————

———————————————————————

———————————————————————

———————————————————————

———————————————————————

Place

Title

Date

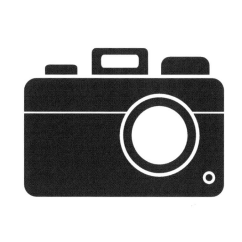

Notes

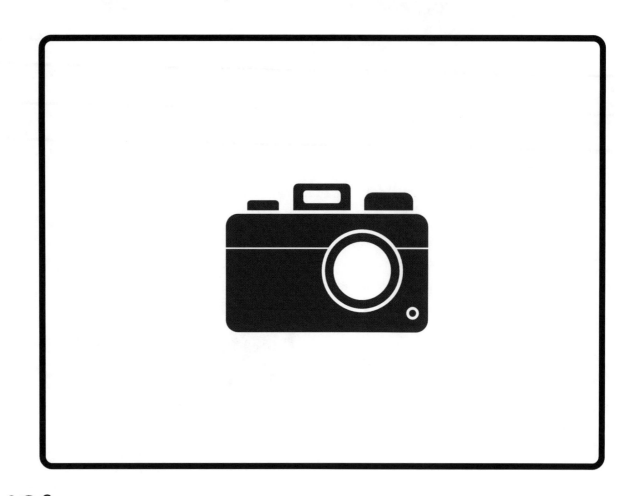

Place _____

Date _____ Title _____

Notes

Place _____

_____

Title _____

_____

Date _____

Notes

_____

_____

_____

_____

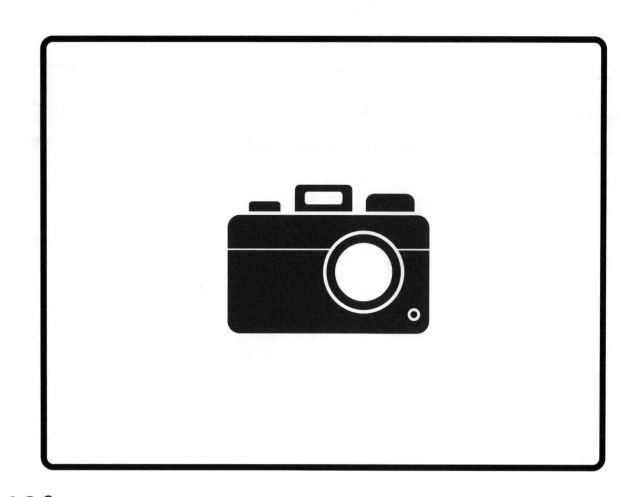

Place _____

Date _____ Title _____

Notes

_____
_____
_____
_____
_____

Place

Title

Date

Notes

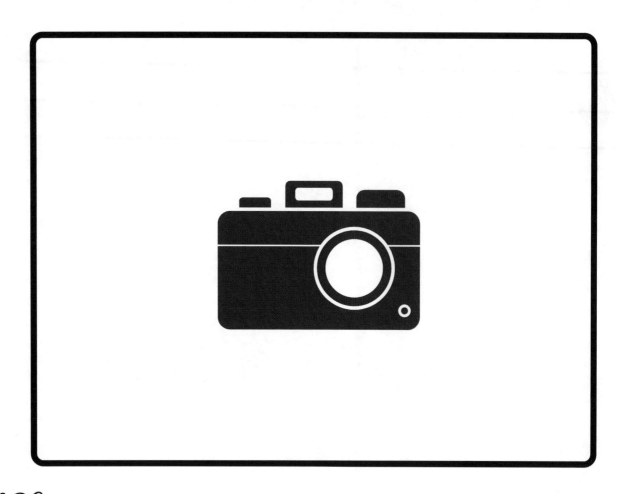

Place ―――――――――――――――――――

Date ――――――― Title ―――――――

Notes

―――――――――――――――――――――――

―――――――――――――――――――――――

―――――――――――――――――――――――

―――――――――――――――――――――――

―――――――――――――――――――――――

Place

Title

Date

Notes

Place ⎯⎯⎯⎯⎯⎯⎯⎯⎯⎯⎯⎯⎯⎯⎯⎯⎯⎯⎯⎯

Date ⎯⎯⎯⎯⎯⎯⎯⎯ Title ⎯⎯⎯⎯⎯⎯⎯⎯⎯

Notes

⎯⎯⎯⎯⎯⎯⎯⎯⎯⎯⎯⎯⎯⎯⎯⎯⎯⎯⎯⎯⎯⎯⎯⎯⎯⎯⎯⎯

⎯⎯⎯⎯⎯⎯⎯⎯⎯⎯⎯⎯⎯⎯⎯⎯⎯⎯⎯⎯⎯⎯⎯⎯⎯⎯⎯⎯

⎯⎯⎯⎯⎯⎯⎯⎯⎯⎯⎯⎯⎯⎯⎯⎯⎯⎯⎯⎯⎯⎯⎯⎯⎯⎯⎯⎯

⎯⎯⎯⎯⎯⎯⎯⎯⎯⎯⎯⎯⎯⎯⎯⎯⎯⎯⎯⎯⎯⎯⎯⎯⎯⎯⎯⎯

⎯⎯⎯⎯⎯⎯⎯⎯⎯⎯⎯⎯⎯⎯⎯⎯⎯⎯⎯⎯⎯⎯⎯⎯⎯⎯⎯⎯

Place

Title

Date

Notes

Place _____

Date _____ Title _____

Notes

_____

_____

_____

_____

_____

Place

Title

Date

Notes

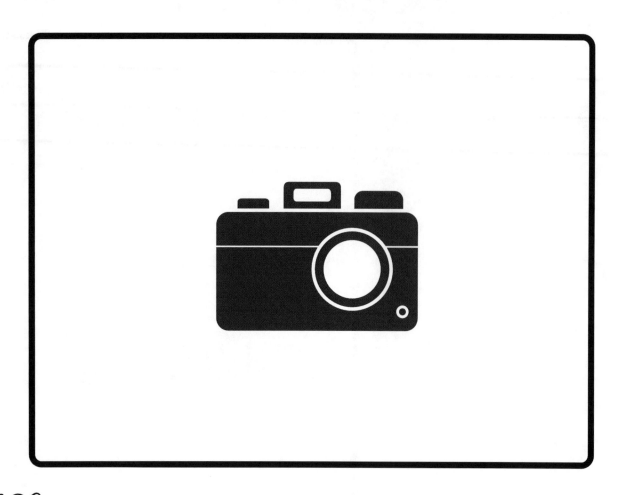

Place ——————————————————————————

Date ———————— *Title* ————————————

Notes

————————————————————————————

————————————————————————————

————————————————————————————

————————————————————————————

————————————————————————————

Place _____

_____

_____

Title _____

_____

_____

Date _____

Notes

_____

_____

_____

_____

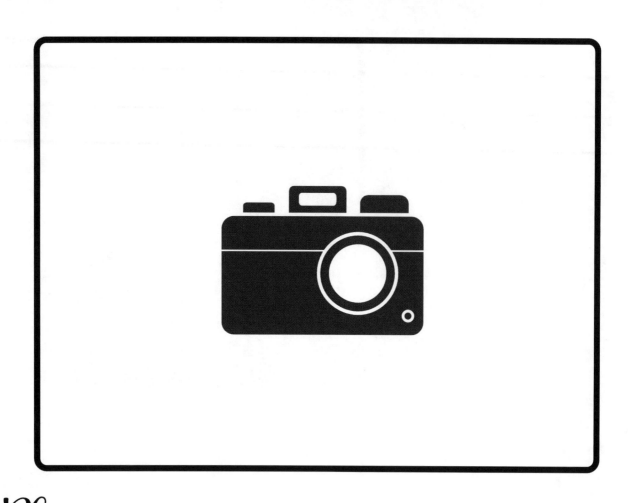

Place _____

Date _____ Title _____

Notes

_____
_____
_____
_____
_____

Place

Title

Date

Notes

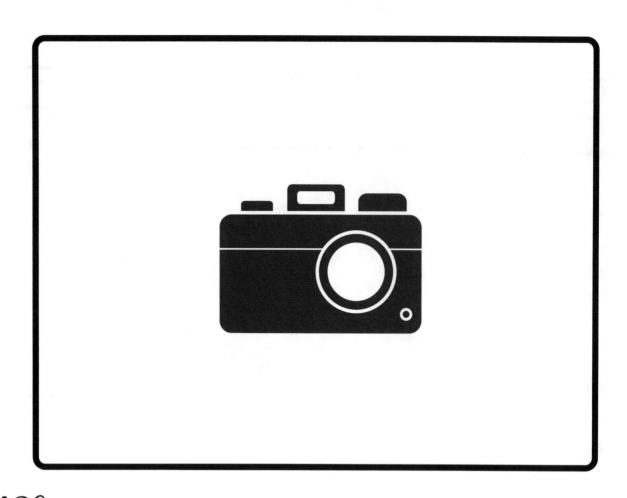

Place _____

Date _____ Title _____

Notes

_____
_____
_____
_____
_____

Place

Title

Date

Notes

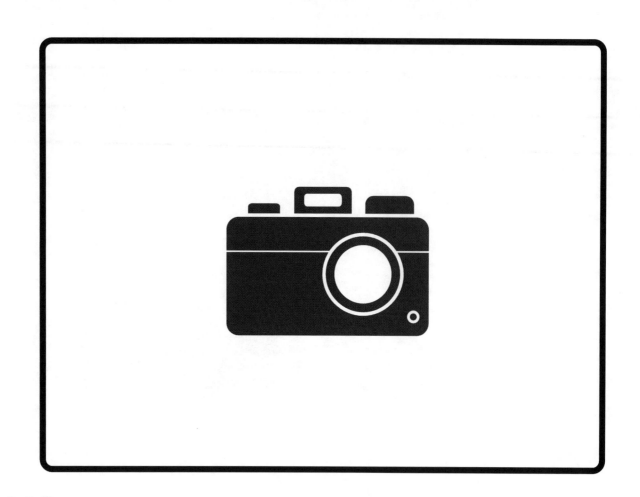

Place _____

Date _____ Title _____

Notes

_____
_____
_____
_____
_____

Place

Title

Date

Notes

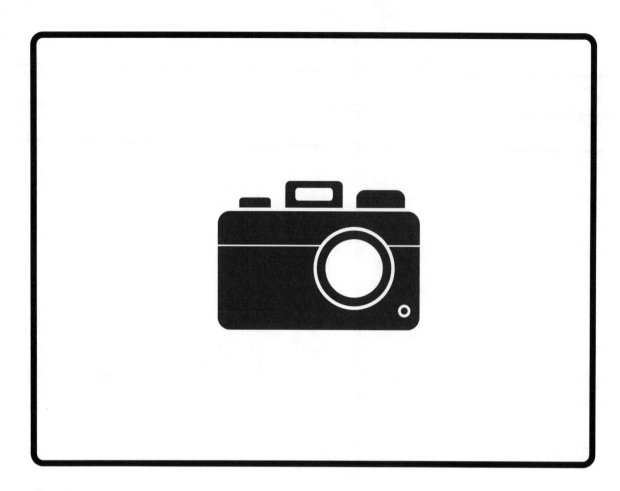

Place ————————————————

Date ———————— *Title* ——————

Notes

————————————————————
————————————————————
————————————————————
————————————————————
————————————————————

Place _____

_____

_____

Title _____

_____

_____

Date _____

Notes

Place —————————————————

Date ——————— *Title* ——————

Notes

————————————————————————

————————————————————————

————————————————————————

————————————————————————

————————————————————————

Place

Title

Date

Notes

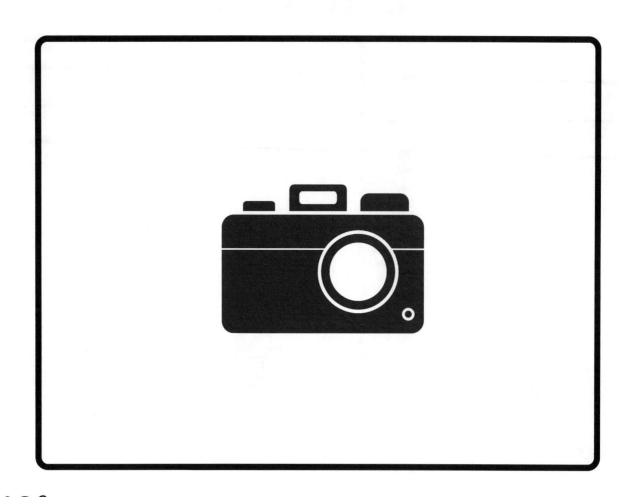

Place _____

Date _____ Title _____

Notes

_____
_____
_____
_____
_____

Place _____

_____

_____

Title _____

_____

_____

Date _____

Notes

_____

_____

_____

_____

Place _____

Date _____ Title _____

Notes

_____

_____

_____

_____

_____

Place

Title

Date

Notes

Place _____

Date _____ Title _____

Notes

_____
_____
_____
_____
_____

Place _____

_____

_____

Title _____

_____

_____

Date _____

Notes

_____

_____

_____

_____

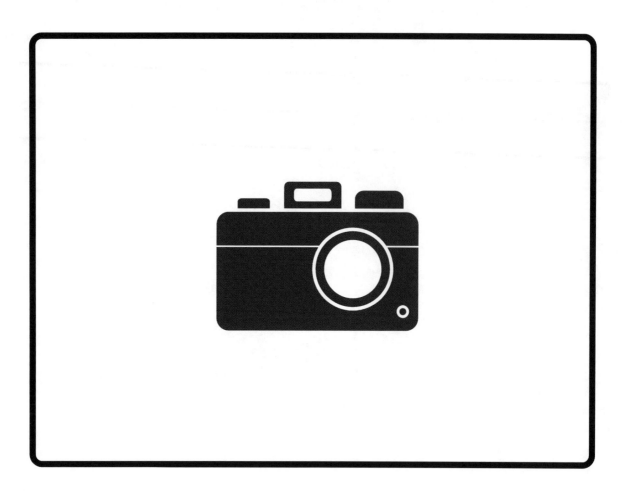

Place _____

Date _____ Title _____

Notes

_____
_____
_____
_____
_____

Place _____

_____

Title _____

_____

Date _____

Notes

_____

_____

_____

_____

Place _____

Date _____ Title _____

Notes

Place

Title

Date

Notes

Place _____

Date _____ Title _____

Notes

_____

_____

_____

_____

_____

Place _____

_____

_____

Title _____

_____

_____

Date _____

_____

Notes

_____

_____

_____

_____

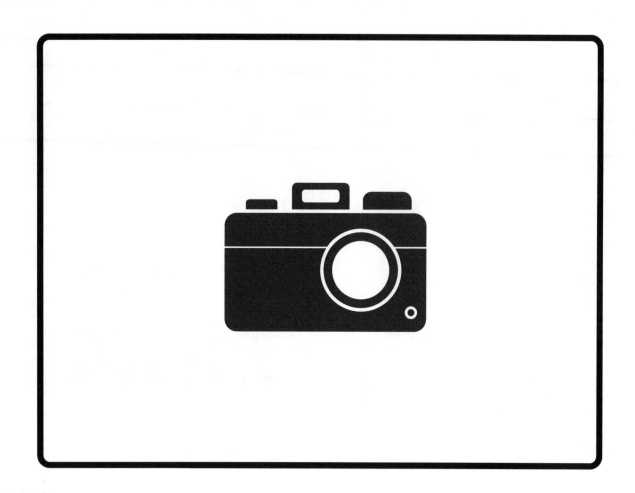

Place _____

Date _____ Title _____

Notes

Place

Title

Date

Notes

Place _____

Date _____ Title _____

Notes

Place

Title

Date

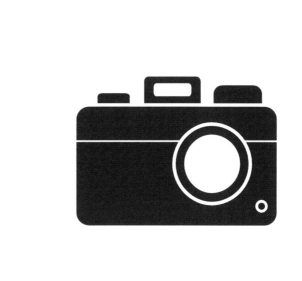

Notes

Place _____

Date _____ Title _____

Notes

Place _____

_____

Title _____

_____

Date _____

Notes

_____

_____

_____

_____

Place _____

Date _____ Title _____

Notes

_____
_____
_____
_____
_____

Place _____

Title _____

Date _____

Notes

Place _____

Date _____ Title _____

Notes

_____

_____

_____

_____

_____

Place _____

_____

Title _____

_____

Date _____

Notes

_____

_____

_____

_____

Place _____

Date _____ Title _____

Notes

_____

_____

_____

_____

_____

Place

Title

Date

Notes

Place _____

Date _____ Title _____

Notes

Place _____

Title _____

Date _____

Notes

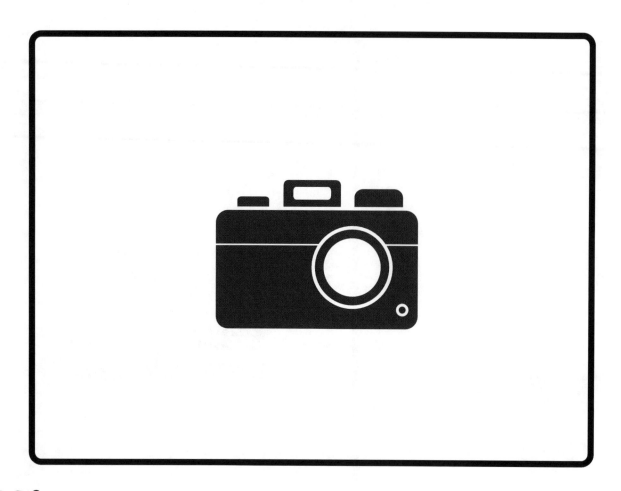

Place _____

Date _____ Title _____

Notes

_____

_____

_____

_____

_____

Place

Title

Date

Notes

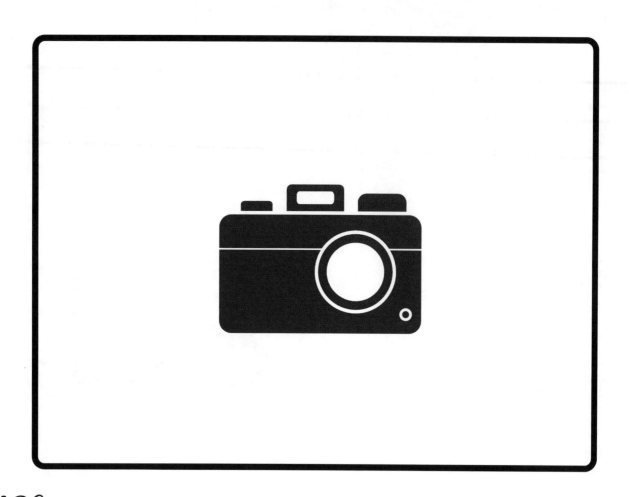

Place _____

Date _____ Title _____

Notes

_____
_____
_____
_____
_____

Place _____

Title _____

Date _____

Notes

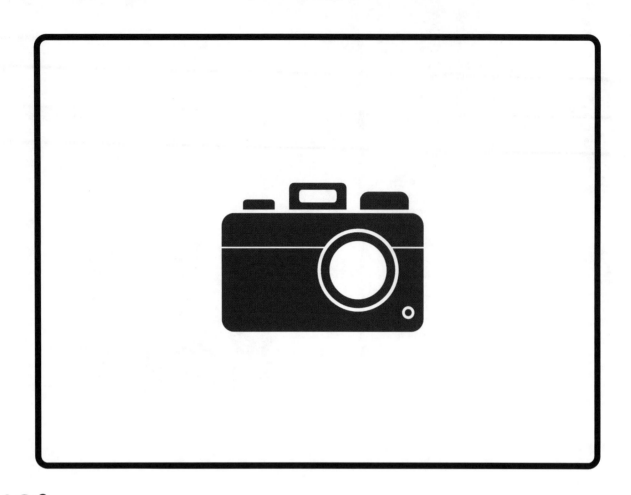

Place _____

Date _____ Title _____

Notes

Place

_____

Title

_____

Date

_____

Notes

Place _____

Date _____ Title _____

Notes

_____
_____
_____
_____
_____

Place

Title

Date

Notes

Place ――――――――――――――

Date ―――― Title ――――――

Notes

Place

Title

Date

Notes

Place ———————————————————————

Date ——————— Title ———————————

Notes

Place

Title

Date

Notes

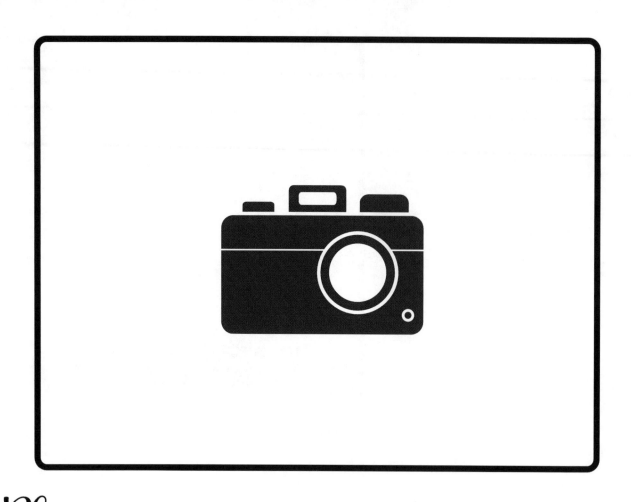

Place _____

Date _____ Title _____

Notes

_____
_____
_____
_____
_____

Made in the USA
Middletown, DE
20 December 2023

46421664R00068